With an Open Heart

With an Open Heart

MICHELLE RIVERA (MIKI)

WITH AN OPEN HEART

This book is written to provide information and motivation to readers. Its purpose is not to render any type of psychological, legal, or professional advice of any kind. The content is the sole opinion and expression of the author, and not necessarily that of the publisher.

Copyright © 2019 by Michelle Rivera (Miki)

All rights reserved. No part of this book may be reproduced, transmitted, or distributed in any form by any means, including, but not limited to, recording, photocopying, or taking screenshots of parts of the book, without prior written permission from the author or the publisher. Brief quotations for noncommercial purposes, such as book reviews, permitted by Fair Use of the U.S. Copyright Law, are allowed without written permissions, as long as such quotations do not cause damage to the book's commercial value. For permissions, write to the publisher, whose address is stated below.

Printed in the United States of America.

ISBN   978-1-64552-093-1   (Paperback)
ISBN   978-1-64552-094-8   (Digital)

Lettra Press books may be ordered through booksellers or by contacting:

Lettra Press LLC
18229 E 52nd Ave.
Denver City, CO 80249
1 303 586 1431 | info@lettrapress.com
www.lettrapress.com

Contents

Many Loves 1
Want to Be 2
Mystery Poem 3
I Don't Want to Die 4
Mother 5
It Is Too Late 6
What to do? It is too late. Nothing Left 7
We Are Different 8
The Sensation 9
Window Open 10
Hard Times 11
Promised 12
We Should 13
Trust 14
Same Routine 15
All We Have 16
Someone 17
Don't Worry 18
Song of Love 19
Into My Mind 20
Miracles 21
The Dentist 22
Free Me 23
What We Are 24
Oh, God 25
Counting Fun 26
Are We Selfish? 27
What Is Going On? 28
Bad Habits 29
My Wish 30
This Is Me 31

Who Is the One?	32
Blood Drops	33
Easy Life	34
About All of You	35
September 4	36
Blind	37
For All of You	38
The Next World	39
Lonely	40
Creative Mind	42
Miracle Hands	43
Irreplaceable	44
Believers	45
How I Feel	46
Why?	48
The Eraser	49
Lovely	50
Missing You	51
I Am Glad	52
You're Unique	53
Let Me Be	54
Belong to You	55
Love Tears	56
Wish	57
Two in One	58
Learn	59
ABC's	60
Look Around	61
Three of Us	62
Trust Me	63
Like Yesterday	64
Without Answer	65
You Are	66
After All	67
Think of Yourself	68
The Solution	69

Celine	70
Silence	71
The Power	72
Tears	73
Is It Worth It to Leave?	74
I Don't Want To	76
You Were the Question	77
Because of You	78
Estranger	79
November 2	80
Hope	81
Never Mind	83
I Will Call You Trash	84
Today is My Day	85
You and Me	86
Looking for You	87
We Believe	88
All I Say	89
A Mistake	90
Don't Be Wrong	91
Can't Forgive You	93
My First Love	94
Four Letters	96
Dreams	97
You Are Still Here	98
Behind You	99
Thank You	100
Liar	101
You Will Not Come	102
You Are Not Alone	103
You Are the One	104
You Are Nothing to Me	105
Your Decision	106
New Year	107
Not Meant to Be	108
Together	109

I Will Tell You	110
Same as You	111
Won't Be Afraid	112
Go On	113
A Real Friend	114
Memories	115
Who Are You?	116
Far Away	118
Thinking About You	119
There Is No Age to Be in Love	120
Love	121
So Sad	122
I Love You	123
Oh, Mother	124
Shining Star	125
Don't	126
Sweet Thoughts	127
Kisses of Wine	128
Painful Love	129
Ghost	130
Nice Day	131
Perfect	132
What a Day	133
I Am a Song	134
No One	135
Christmastime	136
Be Yourself	137
Sounds of My Heart	138
Empty	139
Real or Not Real?	140
Regrets	141
Payback	142
Just Love	143
I May Die	144
The Avoidable	145
What I Said	146

I Can Do It	147
Inspired	148
My Book	149
Holding Our Tears	150
Really Hard	151
My Close Friend	152
What a Dream	153
Come On	154
The Last Page	155
Day by Day	156
Nice Place	157
If You Were Me	158
You Don't Know Me	159
You Are	160
Think About It	161
Expressing	162
Talk About	163
After	164
Sleepless	165
Open Door	166
My Other Half	167
Why?	168
Like a Flower	169
Fantasy Life	170
Mexico's Heart	171
Thinking Like This	172
Poison	173
Like You	174
I Don't Know	175
Wherever You Are	176
Hard to Avoid	177
The Way	178
Is It Magic?	179
Crazy	180
Letting You Go	181
You Are My Reason	182

Happy for You	183
Today	184
My Little Crystal Doll	185
Come to Me	186
Three Wishes	187
Slave	188
Terrible Night	189
Love for Money	190
Show Me the Way	191
Stupid Heart	192
I Am Nervous	193
Same	194
The Past	195
After All	196
Where Are You	197
Don't Trust	198
Believe It	199
You Are	200
Unwanted	201
It Hurts	202
Without Precaution	203
Poet of Love	204
Rain or Tears	205
Human Dog	206
Looking for You	207
All I Am	208
For the Rest of Your Life	209
Am I Dreaming?	210
You and Me	211
Bad Taste	212
Who?	213
Margarita	214

Many Loves

There are many kinds of love.
There might be many more
That I don't know of or I forgot.
The first one is from God.
The second one from your mother,
From the one who gave you birth.
Then, the unconditional love that, when you need it,
Is right there without conditions;
The innocent love, the one that only needs
Hugs and kisses;
And then the dangerous love,
The one with passion, the one with an addiction,
The irresistible one that never thinks,
The one that knows when you are weak
And makes you fall,
The one that makes you believe
In things that don't exist.
And the last one:
The love you can't explain,
But it is real. It's in your heart,
Inside your head; it lives in your mind.
It is willing to live or die just for you.
Love: What a beautiful word love is.

Want to Be

I want to be everything for you.
I want to be you.
I want to be your best friend;
I want to be your lover.
I want to be yours all day.
I want to be your dog
And get your shoes
When you come home.
I want to be your cat.
If you are exhausted,
I will softly rub your back.
I want to be your bed
Where you lie down every night.
I want to be the dreams
You have every night.
I want to be your mirror,
So you can see your reflection in my eyes.
I want to be in your life,
Called by name your wife,
And live forever at your side.

Mystery Poem

I am writing a poem,
But I don't know what about:
Maybe about a friend or a lover.
Maybe about a family or a flower.
Maybe of fear, or a book.
Maybe about me
Or something about you.
Could it be about my singing bird,
Or something from my dog or the world?
Maybe about this life, or just about the stars,
Or about another planet or the moon and the sky.
Or just about my lost cat.
Since this poem is still a mystery,
I will just call it a mystery poem.

I Don't Want to Die

This life is so sweet, like a pie.
This life is splendorous, like the sun.
This life is so bright, like a star.
I don't want to die.
This life is incredible.
This life is so important.
This life is like a beautiful dream.
I don't want to die.
This life is interesting.
There is a lot to learn.
This life exists only one time.
I don't want to die.
I want to stay.
Because we live only once,
I know you can't understand.
I feel so scared.
I don't want to die.
I am begging you.
I hope you read this and let me stay.
This message is for you, God.
I don't want to die.
I am asking you with tears in my eyes
And with hands on my heart.
I need to stay.
I think you know why
I don't want to die.

Mother

To Mom:
Forgive me, Mother,
For all the pain I have caused you
At the time when I was born.
I couldn't do anything
About how much pain you had because of me.
Now I am an adult,
And I will never stop thanking you.
You mean everything to me.
You are always there for me.
I know I don't deserve it
Because sometimes in my life
I failed you, and you always forgave me.
Sometimes I hurt you so much.
Mother, you are unique to me.
You have the biggest heart in the world.
You never see my errors.
You never judge me.
Thank you for being my mother.
I am so grateful to have you.
Be very patient with my craziness.
Thank you for loving me this way.

It Is Too Late

I can't blame it all on you.
It is my fault, too.
My heart was hungry for love
And easy to confuse
After being so damaged
By all those sweet lies,
Fake words, and fake promises.
I still don't understand
Why, if you knew my history,
You decided to stay
And kill me slowly
With your indifference.
You made me believe
That you were not like the others,
That you didn't care about the past.
I should have never waited so long
To know the intentions
That you had on your mind
To use me, and at the same time,
Take advantage of me,
Being fragile and insecure.
I thought that at your side
I may find the window to heaven.
What a shame; you guided me
Through the doors of hell.
It is so unbelievable,
But what is done is done.
Your black heart and my stupidity
Took us so far we will burn in hell.

What to do? It is too late. Nothing Left

I don't have anything to give
But an empty heart,
Waiting for someone out of this world
To fill it out.
I don't have anything to offer,
But I have my poetic mind.
I don't have anything to share,
But I am willing to help.
I don't have anything to show,
But I swear I won't hide anything from you.
I don't have more soul.
I am sorry, but it's not because of you.
I don't have more time,
But I promise I will try it.
I don't have any more life,
But because of you,
I feel like I am reborn.

We Are Different

Far apart we will always be.
We are like oil and water;
We cannot be together.
We are like the sky and the sea,
And the distance is the proof
That we need to understand.
We are like fire and water,
Like love and hate,
Like two enemies,
Like cat and dog,
Like cat and mouse.
Yes, we are like that.
We will never be together,
And there is nothing we can do.
Does it matter anymore?
But we will forever be in love.

The Sensation

You arrived in my life
Like a lost bird.
When I saw you,
I felt my body shake.
When you looked at me,
I felt confident.
When you got close to me, I froze.
When you hugged me, I melted.
When you kissed me,
It felt forbidden.
Now the entire world will know
That you are …
The love of my life.

Window Open

Sometimes, when we don't have hope,
We will find an open door.
Then the circumstances change,
And our dreams become reality.
We will have one tomorrow
That will make us know and learn.
We must never stop,
No matter how hard our life is,
On life's unending road.

Hard Times

When we have an affliction
And our lives are hard to understand,
It is part of our destinies
That know what's best for us.
We all must have faith
And not complain.
After all, destiny will have a better way
To compensate us.
It does not matter how or when.
All we want is to forget
About the hard times
That we have in this life.

Promised

I promised you better days,
And a rainbow after every rainy day.
I promised diamonds and gold
To cover all your needs,
But I won't promise you
If our lives will be good or bad.
That could be a truth or a lie.
Maybe you'll want some more answers
That I cannot provide,
But I know it is a promise
That we'll keep.
I don't know how.
I don't know when.

We Should

We should be more sensible.
We should be more understanding
Toward others.
If someone loves us,
We should be proud to awake
To such a beautiful feeling as love.
We should be honest
And never hurt anyone.
Everyone deserves to dream,
No matter if it becomes a nightmare
Or if it is just a fantasy.
Let them learn.
What is love?

Trust

We should give more and get less.
We can share too.
We should know the importance
Of people around us.
We should look at how important
Our values are.
Nobody is different.
We should see the needs of others.
Let's create a better world
And trust each other,
Like the way it should be.

Same Routine

The clouds are our witnesses:
The nonstopping tears,
The flowers of the garden,
The sound of the river,
The day almost finished.
The night will come along.
This life is the same.
There is nothing new.
It is a routine life,
Always the same thing.
Some things go;
Some things come back.
And we are part of it
Until we are gone
And leave everything behind.
It's like a dream,
Like a fantasy.
We come, we create,
We live, and we die.
And we disappear.

All We Have

The feeling of hope
Comes from the heart.
The faith comes from the hope
That you have within you.
If you find something impossible,
With hope and faith you will get it.
Faith and hope walk together.
Faith and hope are like stars
Illuminating the roads in your life.
Faith and hope are like the moon
That guides your destiny.
Faith and hope are all that matters.
Keep them in your heart.
They are all we have,
Faith and hope.

Someone

Every smile is a feeling of the heart.
Every thought comes with a hope.
Tears hurt
Deep into your soul.
There are moments in your life
That you cannot handle by yourself,
And that is when you need
Someone on your side,
Someone who gives you a hand,
Someone whom you trust,
Someone who loves you
And makes you feel special
No matter who you are.

Don't Worry

Live all you can.
Love much more than you want.
Enjoy all that you have.
Laugh like crazy.
Play like a little kid.
Have fun every day.
Feel grateful for no reason.
Feel the world in your hands.
Touch the sky with your eyes.
Ignore the days and the nights.
Help those who need you.
Tell them not to worry.
Help them to be happy.

Song of Love

Remember those rough days,
How hard our lives were
And how we had to survive,
You in your own way,
And me in my own?
But thanks to destiny,
Our ways become just one road,
And all those days
Are gone,
And our love becomes
A song, a song of love.

Into My Mind

I got into my mind for an instant
And asked myself a question.
How would I write a book
That would express my feelings?
Would everybody read it?
Would it go around the world?
Would it be known?
Would someone like it?
Would it be important?
Should I die to be important?
Would it be an important book?
I wish to know,
But no matter what happens,
I will write it anyway,
And it will be in God's hands.
I hope it touches the heart
Of everybody, one by one.
You don't need to make it famous.
I just hope you read it.

Miracles

I know miracles exist.
I am waiting for one.
Every morning when I open my eyes,
I have hope.
I know it will come.
Sooner or later, I will be better;
Then my brain will heal,
My bones will be strong,
My feet will get stronger.
My heart will be without pain
And hold a bigger faith.
Miracles really exist.
I know it's hard to believe,
But I do know it will come.

The Dentist

"Like a shiny smile,
Like to be on file."
This is what my dentist says
When I get my cleaning done.
And this is what I say:
"It is better to have
A happy face,
With a happy smile
And a brighter day."
Walking on the street,
Showing my whiter teeth,
I made the right choice.
I could not complain.
I have one of the best,
A perfect place.
I will be patient until next time,
As a patient, when I visit
My dentist again.

Free Me

I love to be
Free like the ocean,
Free like a river,
Free as air.
I love to be
Free like a song,
Free like time,
Free like liberty,
Free as a flying bird.
I loved to be free …

What We Are

I am not
More than you are.
You are not
More than I am.
They are not
More than we are.
We are not
More than anybody is.
We are just whatever
We want to be.
Who can argue about that?
That is what you are.
This is what I am.

Oh, God

God gave me wings to fly to you,
But I am afraid.
God gave me two feet
To walk closer to you,
But I forgot how.
God gave me a brain to
Imagine you,
But I can't.
God gave me
An enormous heart to love you,
But you broke it.
God gave me two eyes to see you,
But they can't find you.
God gave me two hands
To touch you,
But I don't know, or
What to do with them.
God gave me a beautiful soul.
I hope I can always keep it
Away from you.

Counting Fun

One, two, three,
I am always free.
Four, five, six,
Come on, please.
Seven, eight, nine,
Make up your mind.
Ten, eleven, twelve,
Tell me where.
Thirteen, fourteen, fifteen,
I am your queen.
Sixteen, seventeen, eighteen,
We are a team.
As kids, we like to count;
We like to play.
Let's keep counting
Till the end of this game.

Are We Selfish?

Why are we so selfish,
And hurt others
Just because of what we want?
Sometimes we hear
What we want to hear,
And not what is true.
We are not perfect,
So before we complain,
We should think twice.
That way, we don't hurt others.
Let's value more what
We have and not push it away;
Make it happy, not miserable.
Let's take advantage of all the love
That they feel for us.
So before we think of ourselves,
Let's think of others first.
Let's close our eyes and
Love them back the way they love us.

What Is Going On?

God, oh God, what is going on?
A lot of people around me,
They make me nervous.
I think they don't like me.
But they are right;
I've become a family
Without being one of them.
But why do they blame me?
It's not my fault we fall in love.
So the guilty are our hearts.
Thanks to them, we have no choice.
The heart is like a kid;
It's blind, never sees what it's going to do.
The sooner we fall in love.

Bad Habits

Lying is the most common habit
Of those that we, as humans, have.
But have you ever thought
Why are we liars?
In my point of view,
I think that when we are born,
We get raised
With what you call
Errors and defects.
Because nobody is perfect.
And if you think you are,
You are wrong.
At least once in your life,
You did it; big or small,
It doesn't matter.
It is lying, and sometimes
We are able to do it
Because we have been hurt
And life forces us to do it,
And that is the only defense we have.
We use it for protection
When we have been
Treated like trash.
We need at least two lives
To forget about it.
I hope you understand.
If you know love,
Then you know pain.

If God would ask me
What do I want to be in my next life?
I would answer fast and with happiness:
I would like to be the wind
Because it is created for you.
It is part of the universe,
And it never dies.
It's everywhere,
Blowing softly and hard.
Caressing and hugging.
And it is a witness to everything.
It likes to whistle and whisper.
It is subtle and strong
In all existing ears.

This Is Me

This would be my last thought,
But you'll never know.
I just want to tell you
Something about me.
My book is like an open door to my heart.
I am so romantic, sensitive,
And sentimental.
I believe in every person.
I know there is hope
For everything.
I believe in faith,
I believe in love,
I believe in God,
I believe in me.
In writing this book,
I wanted to share my thoughts
Around the world and leave
A piece of my heart in everyone,
Like a memory that never dies.
I don't care if I am
In the last place on earth
And my name appears
With the smallest letters in this universe
Or in another language.
You are my heart; you are my wings.
Take me around the world.
Spread my book.
My love and your heart
Is the same as mine.

Who Is the One?

Who is the one that always waited for you?
The one that begged so much,
The one that cried just for you,
The one that gave up everything for you?
Who is the one who believed in all your lies?
The one that you ignored all your life,
The one that you confused really well,
The one that you never cared about?
Who is the one that never gave up?
The one that looked at you like a god ?
The one that lived life like a dream
And didn't want to wake up?
Who is the one that will kill the stupid feelings,
The one that everybody calls the first love,
The one that confused us with the wrong one
Until we find the right one?
Who is the one that now knows the truth,
The one that is smarter than you
And decided that you are worthless?
Do you want to know who is the one?
That one is me, the one who learned
How to take you out of my heart.

Blood Drops

How far can the mind go?
How far can love travel?
How deep can we hurt someone
Without thinking of what the consequences are,
So deep that their soul will bleed
With pain dripping in each drop of blood,
Making their soul die slowly?
Who is to blame, the brain or the heart?
I would like to know.
Which one makes us go so far
As doing terrible things for love?

Easy Life

Once again hear my words:
The door is open if you want to go.
I let you go. You are free.
Go and talk to the world.
What you felt for me wasn't love.
Swallow your pride
And tell the truth.
Talk to them like you did to me
About a better life without worry,
About tomorrow, about today.
And in case you want to change your mind,
Don't bother. It is too late.
And let me tell you,
Yes, I want you,
But not here. Stay away,
As far away as you can,
And stay right there.
Once again, you are free.
I don't want you to be my fear.
It's not a big deal; there are more like you
That think they're smart.
I know I'm not dumb,
And as far as I know,
I am done with you.
Sometimes there is someone
Who makes you see
What you don't want to see.

About All of You

Oh my, oh my,
There you are,
All of you working hard.
Oh my, oh my, nonstop.
You never stop.
How incredible, all of you,
A good team, a perfect one.
No need for a lead, no need for a guide,
Fallowing orders,
Just from your beautiful heart.

September 4

September 4, September 4.
My sweetheart, my princess, the only one,
The one with the biggest heart,
The one that never asks
And always has free time to give,
And true love to expand.
September 4, September 4,
An unforgettable holiday.
What a day, what a day,
When I got my little one in my arms.
For the first time in the world,
I couldn't say a single word;
I wasn't able to understand.
What I felt—I just wanted to cry
That day when you were born,
On September 4.

Blind

This is a poem for you, or you and only you.
I don't know how to describe you.
I thought I knew you so well
Until I saw so much sadness
And loneliness in your eyes,
And I find out how many times
Your heart as been broken.
There are no more tears to waste.
I don't understand how you let
Those bad people
Break your life into pieces
And never let you be happy,
Having a normal life.
Everybody moves you up, down, side to side,
And you are still holding there.
Everybody cuts your heart in half,
And you are still smiling, sitting next to them.
If someone lies to you today,
Tomorrow you'll believe in another one.
If your love throws you out,
There you are the next day helping them,
Giving them all you have.
Sorry, but you are blind.
You need to wake up, close your heart,
And say, forgive me, God.
I hope there is no punishment for being blind
And something else that I might deserve:
For not being mature enough
And knowing the world enough.

For All of You

Everybody is a poet,
But nobody knows how to express a feeling
When the heart talks.
Or maybe they are afraid
Of what a poet feels.
Being a poet is kind of hard.
Is not you anymore;
It is your heart that really talks.
You become the love.
You become the feeling of others.
You become the air, the stars,
The sky, the day or the night.
With the moon and the sun, there is no more you.
There is only a book that keeps your heart,
That keeps your soul,
And is called the book of love.
Giving everybody a different story,
A different way to love someone,
With an open heart,
Finding a beautiful thing
That was never seen before
But was there.
A book of love is one that teaches
Words of love and feelings.
For those who want to love,
A book of love is what you need.

The Next World

Someone says life is like a book,
But I have my own opinion.
Life is like being asleep
And having
Two kinds of dreams:
Sweet dreams when you're happy
And nightmares when you suffer,
For some reason or someone,
Like having someone on your side
And feeling lonely.
Sweet dreams when you feel
Someone close to you, even if they are far away.
It doesn't matter; with true love,
There is no distance.
Remember, dreaming is like being in heaven;
Nightmares are like being stuck in hell.
Sweet dreams or not, have a long, long sleep
Until the day comes and you must wake up
To the reality of the real world that nobody knows.

Lonely

Sitting on a black chair, close to the window
On the third floor of a lonely place,
Some sad souls are looking for some company.
Someone to listen to their problems.
Someone to make them feel alive again.
It is a place like a lost world
With a lot of people, but nobody can see you,
Where you see a window like an escape door,
Which makes you realize,
I could be awake for a second,
And I could be living this reality
Just by closing my eyes and trying to fly.
But somehow, at those moments
Is when you became the smartest one
And used your brain, smarter than your heart,
And started to read the book of your life,
Starting from the first day of your life.

The beautiful book is your major treasure,
Your best friend, the one who knows you better,
The one who keeps your secrets,
And it is so much to read it makes you learn
Until you understand that you are the one
Who chose to live in a dream,
Or dream like you are living.
Live, use your brain,
But don't forget your heart.
It is a dumb heart,
But it is a sweet heart too.
There are no better friends
Than brain and heart.

Creative Mind

All I can say about your experience is,
You only need a creative mind.
I am very sure that what your hands
Start to touch, it won't be the same.
I don't know you very well,
And I believe I don't need to
Because your enthusiasm talks for you.
You have not finished yet, and it looks great already.
Closing my eyes, I can see what a job you have done.
It is like you knew what I wanted.
What a place, what a sight,
And what an expert you are.
I am very sure that the world
Has an open door for you
With a room full of people
Wanting to congratulate you
For being so creative in what you do.

Miracle Hands

Thank you, God.
Thank you, God.
I never thought you would put me
In the hands of a beautiful angel
While you were taking care of me.
Thank you for putting in him a beautiful heart,
For guiding his mind and hands.
Following you, he brought my baby to this world
And brought me back to life.
I wish the best for all your followers
Who take seriously their lifetime of study.
Thank you again, and don't forget
Your preferred angel
With miracle hands.

Irreplaceable

Oh, no—what a dark place.
There is no more sunlight.
There is no more sunlit garden.
It so sad, missing a wonderful friend,
The one that without question offers help.
It is an empty place without you.
Oh, no—it won't be the same
Without your help, without a friend.
There is no one who can replace you.
They may try, but it won't be the same
As when you have a friend you can call family,
Someone that is just irreplaceable.

Believers

By looking up to the sky,
I asked some questions to God.
Oh God, my true friend,
My feelings, my ears,
My voice, my words:
Is it possible to send you
A message with the pope?
I know you are here, always next to me,
And if you let me touch your holy hand,
It would be a wonderful feeling in my heart.
I want to be blessed by you.
So once again make me humble.
Make me heal, cleanse my body,
Cleanse my heart, and cleanse my soul.
Take away all the sins
That my dark side hid.
Oh God, oh God,
Let me feel the Holy Spirit
And receive your blessings
With a touch of your hands.

How I Feel

I could explain how or what I feel,
But I don't know how.
I am so confused.
In an instant, I feel happy.
In the next, I am crying,
Or I become filled with laughter.
I must be crazy.
One day I feel like smiling and talking,
And the next day I find everything gray.
I have people around me, yet I feel alone,
Walking around without being heard,
Without being seen.
It is like I am invisible even if I talk.
It is so hard being like this.
Should I laugh, or should I cry?
What a name for a song.
I guess I sound funny right now.
But at a time like this
Is when you need your guts.

WITH AN OPEN HEART

Don't give up. Be your own hero.
Be your own example.
If people without feet
can move around, so can you.
If people without hands
can do things, so can you.
Be strong; it is all you need.
No matter how long you live,
Live it completely,
Like you've never done it before.
Be a little selfish. Be nice to yourself.

Why? Why? Why don't you understand
That the love that I have is just for you?
Why? Why? Why does it look
Like you don't care a bit for me?
Why? Why? Why is all you care for
The satisfaction of your body?
Why? Why? Why do you never follow your heart?
Why? Why? Why do you always complain
For the minimal reason that you always have?
Why? Why? Why do you never ask for what I need
Or tell me that you are there for me?
Why? Why? Why did you forget
All the details you used to know?
Is it because the love that you had for me
Wasn't true? It was all fake, same as you.
Why? Why? Why do we never talk
Or discuss certain points?
Why? Why? Why do you have the right
To do all that you want,
And I have to ask, knowing you will never agree?
Why? Why? Why are you the one
Who always punishes me?
Is it because I am older than you?
Could it be fear?
Let me tell you, for when I am gone,
There won't be sorries, only questions.
Why? Why? Why?

The Eraser

I wish to be the biggest eraser that exists
So that I can erase all the love that is in my heart,
All those prints that your kisses left on my lips,
All those marks that your hands put all over my body,
All those words that you whispered in my ear,
All those nights when your love
Became the most beautiful promise that I knew.
Erase your name, erase those eyes
That make me fall for you,
The fake of your actions.
Erase those thoughts that I have in my mind.
I want to stop thinking always about you
And bring back all the sleep that I lost,
All those nights dreaming about you,
Erase the long, long time
That I wasted on you.
Erase the road where I found you,
The day when I made the worst choice in my life,
Thinking that you were an angel
Without knowing how diabolical you were.
You must have a rock instead of a heart,
Doing things without care,
Like destroying the life of more than one.

Lovely

I never thought how lovely
It feels to be in your strong arms,
Feeling the warmth of your body,
Forgetting the time of day and place.
It doesn't matter if it is in a palace.
It doesn't matter if it is in the desert.
It is so lovely being next to you.
It doesn't matter how long;
What matters is this moment
When I feel that I am alive,
And I feel, and I hear.
Tasting your kisses
With the best, softly fine wine
That you ever have.
It is so lovely being here, you and me,
For the first time or the last.
I don't care; I just don't think
About the past, about what's next.
The past is the past; the future, who knows?
What counts is that we are now,
Right here and right now.

Missing You

Oh my, oh my, oh my,
You just left, and I miss you already.
I would like to make the time shorter,
Or at least cut it in half.
Oh no, oh no, oh no,
Please hurry up.
Don't forget, I can't breathe
When you're gone.
I can't sleep if you don't come.
Please come; I can't wait.
I may die if you take too long.
Oh well, oh well, I'll hang on.
I will try to survive
Until you come back.

I Am Glad

What the heck? What's this?
Is it because of you,
Or is it because of me?
Is it new, what I feel?
I didn't know
This kind of feeling.
Every time when I hear your name,
I have shaky hands.
Every time I hear about you,
I feel butterflies all over me.
Every time I see your eyes,
My heart beats hard,
And it makes me so nervous
If you're too close.
What the heck? I would like to know
If we need a touch of our lips to find out
If this is the magic word,
That magic feeling called love.
If it is so, I am glad.
What I feel is love,
And it is for you.
Just for you.

You're Unique

Don't ever forget what you mean to me.
I'm very sure you know it.
Since I found my world in you,
My life changed; you became part of me.
You're my happiness.
You're the most important person in my life.
I love every part of you:
Your sense of humor,
Your laughs with a simple joke,
Those sweet looks in your eyes
And such beautiful feeling in your heart.
You're unique; I find so much in you,
Leaning on your side, little by little,
Until we become just one soul
Full of us, full of love.
As you can see,
Neither you nor me,
We won't forget, not today, not tomorrow.
We always will be two in one.
What is done is done.

Let Me Be

Let me take you as far as I can.
Let me cure your heart and soul.
Let me hug you with my warm arms.
Let me get inside of your confused mind.
Let me tell you the sweetest words.
Let me earn your trust again.
Let me convince you
That this is not your end.
Let me treat you like myself.
Let me be on your side.
Let me share your dreams.
Let me stay in your life.
Let me be the best part of your life.
Let me be the last one
Who stays inside your heart,
And together, let us laugh, dream, and sing.
Leave the past behind,
And be like we are in another world.
Our world, our own world.

Belong to You

I see you today like never before.
My heart can't stop; it's only for you.
My lips felt so warm
The first time that you came.
I never forgot
Because the minute I saw you,
You were in my head.
The second day, you stuck in my heart,
And we all know that
That's your place.
In case you want to leave,
My body will die.
Since the day I met you,
Your hands have been holding my life.
Be generous with me, and let me
Give you all that I have.
Be honest with me.
I don't care if I'm going to die,
Because if I die for you,
You will never forget
How I'm feeling for you.
Love, love is what I have for you.
Please don't let me go.
My soul belongs to you,
And all of me is just for you.

Love Tears

I miss your laughs;
I miss your hugs.
Tattoos of your touch are all I have.
If you come soon, I'll wait for you.
If you come late, I won't be here.
If you love me so, I cry for you,
But don't be sad—tears of love.
So I bless your soul,
and I live with hope.
I miss your face when you get mad,
How sometimes you got so nervous,
How your cheeks become so red
That you could not talk.
I miss you; I love you so.
Don't let me drown in tears of love.

I close my eyes and feel the air.
I hold your hand; you are still here.
You make me upset when I don't see you.
I'm here for you, and you don't care.
But we will see what comes next.
That's why I don't have any fear
Of losing all that I never had.
I wish I knew the only way
To take you out of my life.
By keeping a closed mind and heart,
You make me feel like trash,
And with all of that, I will give up.
After all, you are not the only one.
There is someone who needs,
Someone else to give love to.
So from now on, the door to my heart
Is closed for you, and there is no key
For you to ever open by you, ever.

Two in One

Here I am. Take my heart, take my soul,
Take me all, make me laugh, play with me.
Be there for me anytime, anywhere.
Give me peace; give me love.
Let me have faith in you.
Let me dream. Take me high,
Really high into the sky;
Let me wander through the stars.
Let me believe I can fly.
Come to me, come with me.
We won't walk; we will run holding hands.
We will run together, forever and ever in love,
For what we feel will never end.
Give me a kiss; take my lips.
I want to experience your sweet taste.
Feel the warmth of my breath.
Make it once, make it twice, please don't stop—
As you know, we must tell the world,
From now on, how our love
Will become two in one.

.

Learn

You broke my heart; that's all I know.
You make me sad when you say no.
I feel strong if you are with me.
It's a shame I have to leave.
All you see is all I have.
Once you decide to change your mind,
Come back to me and learn to love.
It's hard for you; it's hard for me.
I have the moon, I have the sky,
And all the stars are just for you.
All day, all night, all day, all noon.
Enjoy the view so you learn from me
And I learn from you.
Please love me so, and I'll love you too.

ABC's

A, B, and C, come right here;
Come and see.
D, E, and F, let's go play.
G, H, and I are my friends.
J, K, and l come to dance.
Let's go; join us.
M, N, and O, jump once;
Let's all jump again.
P, Q, and R, here you are;
Let's go count.
S, T, and U, follow me to the ground;
Feel the grass.
W, X, and Y, give me a ride.
Don't go too fast!
I get scared, but I have fun.
Z is the last letter,
The end of the game.
If you want to learn,
Let's play again.
After all, ABC's
Are our friends.

Look Around

My heart beats for you;
My mind is out of me.
It's great, what I feel, but it's
Something I don't like.
I know it's really late
To run away from you.
My feet will walk away;
My life will stay with you.
It's so easy for you to fall in love;
Why not with me?
It's so hard for me to tell my heart
To be strong and forget about your love.
Don't be blind; open your eyes.
Look all around, and you will see
Who is for you.

Three of Us

It was a dark night;
It was a beautiful night.
You and me, sitting at the front door,
Counting the stars one by one—
You were there, still with me.
After all, with all the love
That God saw in us,
He decided to complete our lives
With a lovely child.
And now and then,
We will not be alone.
We are complete,
Forever you, forever me,
Forever us three and our love
That will never end.
And God's love, that we will always have,
With heart and soul.
This becomes our fate.

Trust Me

Like rain are your tears.
Like a lie is your pain.
Hope is your word;
I know your sorrow.
Don't tell me that you regret what you did.
That's the way we have to learn.
No matter what, no matter who,
It always hurts.
Please, trust me for once—trust me now.
Only time will talk for you.
Please be bright; please be strong.
I will be with you, on your side.
You will never be away from me.
Never alone, always with me.
Always with me.

Like Yesterday

It has been twenty-five years,
And it looks just like yesterday
When I met you.
I remember how shy you were.
Your cheeks always turned red
Whenever you tried to talk to me.
I can't forget our first date
And the following dates after that,
The beautiful flowers I got from you.
In our first month, you wrote me a song.
In our first six months, you drew me a picture.
In our first year, you wrote a poem for me,
And then my love for you grew much more.
And that's why the world belongs to us,
Because both of us are strong.
You love me, and I love you more,
And our love will never end.
Loving you is my life;
Having you is my gift.
So here we are today.
Our love will never end.

Without Answer

Sitting under a beautiful tree,
Looking at the moon,
I asked myself, why did I let you go?
Why did I not stop you?
Why did I not tell you how much I loved you?
Why did I not tell you how much I care for you?
Why did I not open my heart
So you could see right through me?
Why did I waste so much time ignoring you?
There are so many questions with no answer.
I should not have kept my feelings hidden,
But I was afraid to be disappointed.
So now, I am not so sure if I did right
Or if I did wrong. I don't know.
All I know is
I should've never let you go.

You Are

You are the moon of my nights.
You are the sun of my mornings.
You are the destiny in my life.
You are my only lovely love.
Your lips taste like sweet wine.
You are unique in my heart.
You are all the words of this world.
You are the mystery of my soul
And the answer without question.
You are the visible and invisible.
You are the one
Who makes me happy in this world.
You are my all, after all.
You are so beautiful, like a garden.

After All

After all the love
I gave to you,
You are gone again.
After sharing so much with you,
You are leaving without me.
After all, I lost everything for you,
And you pay me like this.
After how much I have loved you,
You forgot about me.
After I thought that you were only mine,
You are finished with me today.
After I swear to love you forever,
You hurt me so much.
After I support you,
You take away all my happiness.
After all my sacrifice,
You kick me out of your life.
After being your shadow,
I changed my mind and will leave you alone
And give you a well-deserved goodbye.

Think of Yourself

If you are sad, think of yourself.
When you are happy, do it for you.
When you have a dream,
Keep it for you.
When you don't believe in anybody,
Believe in yourself.
If you are lost, find yourself.
When nobody loves you,
Love yourself.
When you want someone to love you,
Love yourself first.
When you fall, get up and continue.
When you want to know your worth,
Check your qualities.
When nobody understands you,
Understands yourself first.
When you have lost all hope,
It's because you need to have faith.
If you lost all your faith,
You need God.
When you have God with you,
You don't need anything else.

The Solution

I have three friends—
My mind, my heart, my soul—
And all of them confuse me.
My heart says that
You are the man of my life.
My soul says, "Don't listen to your heart."
My mind thinks about the passion.
Then I say to myself,
"Life is too short, and
You have to live it."
Then my heart says,
"You are right."
My mind has a suggestion:
"Let's all three make an effort.
Let's put our mind, heart, and soul
Into this thing called love."

Celine

Celine is your name,
And I am going to describe it.
You are the reason of my life.
I am so glad you are here.
You are the queen of any king.
You are the owner of this world.
The universe belongs to you.
Celine, a sweet name,
A celestial one, a lucky one.
A name that comes from the sky,
Sent from God just for you.
Celine, a beautiful name.

Silence

How horrible silence is.
It is like a dark hole,
Dusty and lonely.
So dark, where the light
Never comes out.
Same as silence,
Where nobody will talk.
Dusty and in ruins.
Silence will always be there,
Same way the heart is feeling.
Because since then,
Since you left me years ago,
My heart only cries and cries,
And in darkness
My heart will die.

The Power

I throw my memories to the sea,
And I put a stone on my heart.
I throw your kisses to the air,
And I lie to the mirror,
And I ask God for advice.
God gives me a million opinions,
But he gives me some conditions.
He tells me, "Go to the sea,
and pick up your memories.
Then I will convert them into poems.
Take out the stone out of your heart.
There I will put a diamond instead.
Tell yourself you are sorry
In front of the mirror,
And you will find a real friend."

Tears

How sad it is to see
The mountains dry,
Imploring for water.
You may not hear their voices,
But they are screaming for rain.
They don't want to die;
They want to keep on living.
They need their green color
And the perfume of their flowers
And the wind to spread it
To those who really love it.

Is It Worth It to Leave?

I want to tell you goodbye
In case tomorrow I can't.
Maybe I won't be here,
And the happiness in your eyes
I want to take with me.
I ask you to take care of me
When I really need it;
I beg you, don't suffer for me
And keep my soul in your heart.
I wish I could stay till eternity for you.
I would like to decide, but I have no choice.
When I am already gone,
Don't cry for me.
Only two things I want from you:
To protect with all your heart
The one we created with love.
Don't let her get hurt,
And be there always for her.
Never forget about me.

Take me always with you,
Like if I were here with you.
Forgive me for not continuing.
My eyes are full of tears,
And I can't write anymore.
I hope, when that happens,
The years are already gone
So I can ask God to let me stay
A hundred years with you.
Then I will be ready to go.

I Don't Want To

I don't want your love.
I don't want you to be sorry for me.
I don't want anything from you.
I don't want to see you or hear you.
I don't want to share my sadness.
Your presence bothers me.
I don't want to know
If you care about me.
Just leave; just go.
You don't mean anything
To me anymore.

You Were the Question

Your letters were so romantic,
It looked like they were alive.
You were so different
From far away.
You had more details
Without saying a word.
In front of people,
You were a gentleman.
You never trusted me.
When I asked about something,
Instead of answering,
You had another question.
You made me so confused.
For all the time I was with you,
I doubted if you really loved me.
Sometimes you did,
But I'd better not ask
Because my answer
Will be another question.

Because of You

You don't know
How hard it is for me
To write about you.
You are not easy to describe.
How do I get to know
Who you are?
This is a gift that I want for you.
Read it and you will know
The secret that I hide.
You will find that the one
Who lives in my heart is you.
You give me inspiration
To write a romantic book.

Estranger

How can I tell
If you really love me
If I don't have you?
You don't have time for me.
Your friends are first.
I don't know what is wrong.
You are not the same person I met years ago,
The one who used to say sweet words
And gave me beautiful looks.
But no more.
Today I have decided to put an end,
An end to this nightmare.
And if you are okay or not,
I don't care.
I will just ask myself,
Why did I wait so long?
I will never forgive myself for this.
I wasted my life, just for you.
But it is never too late.
There is always someone waiting for you,
A real person, a real love,
A real heart, a real soul,
Someone who has beautiful feelings,
Someone who knows
How valuable a person I am.
Goodbye, stranger,
And thank you for nothing.
What else can I say to you?
You are worth nothing.

November 2

November 2 is a special day
For us and for them,
Those who made the last step,
Going to a better place.
They are happy, and we are still sad.
We still feel they are here,
That they're not dead.
We know how hard this is,
But sooner or later,
We will go there too.
It sounds horrible,
But that's the road we can't avoid.
I wish we could change the road.
But the more I think,
There is not another way.
We'd better be good,
We'd better be kind
And follow the road of life,
And all we need to do is pray and pray
So that on our last step to a better life,
God will be there with open hands
And open heart and lovely voice.
He will say to each one of us, in different ways,
Words of love we will understand.

Hope

Do I give up? Do I have hope?
It is so big, my pain that I don't understand.
I wish I knew magic. I wish today was yesterday.
I wish I could go back and start all over again.
I know I'm strong, but I don't want to do it.
I know I'm smart, but I prefer to ignore it.
I know I can do it, but I don't want to try it.
I feel that there is only one day that I have to live.
It seems like there is no tomorrow for me.
I must be wrong, but I don't care.
Maybe these are yesterday words.
Today I saw a man without legs,
And he had a happy face.
The other day I saw a girl with no arms,
And she was laughing nonstop.
This morning I saw a blind person
Walking alone and singing a beautiful song.
And right now I'm looking at the mirror,
And talking to myself, I say,
"I can walk, I can see, and I can touch my nose.
I must have hope; I don't need to give up.
I'm going to fight. I'm going to be happy.

I'm going to give all the love that I still have to my loved ones
So on the day that I do have to go,
All my loved ones can remember me with a happy face."
But anyway, I will never leave.
You might not see me,
But I will be here
Next to all those who gave me love,
Next to the ones I love, the ones who cared for me.
So I will be here, forever around, with hope.

Never Mind

I always say,
You are not the first,
You are not the last,
But you are the one
who breaks my heart.
And not only that,
You let my soul die.
And you are the only one
Who makes me feel like this.
I never thought
You would run away with another one.
I have no more trust.
You know you are my life, you are my sun,
You are my morning star,
And I could be your shining moon, just for you.
But don't worry.
I'm strong, and I will be right here,
Waiting just for you,
With open arms and open heart.
As you know, you are the only one who lives in me,
The only one who breaks my heart,
The only one who will fix it back.
I know you will be back.

I Will Call You Trash

You are the error of my life.
You are my worst nightmare.
You are the one who changed my destiny.
You are the one who makes me a bad person.
You are the one who shows me the wrong roads.
You are the one who kills all my feelings.
You are the one who makes me feel dirty.
You are the darkness of my soul.
You are the one who poisoned my love.
You are the one who takes away all my faith.
You are the one who never stands for me.
So hold right there—don't take any more steps.
You are the one who nobody wants to be next to.
You are just trash to me.

Today is My Day

I love the cloudy days.
I like the rainy nights.
In the cloudy days,
I have your warm hugs.
In the rainy nights,
I have your sweet lips.
The rain makes us dream
Of you and me.
The cloudy days give us peace;
They give us trust.
I like the sunny days too.
Why not? They're warm and lovely,
Like you and me,
And sometimes so hot,
Giving us those days we won't forget.
Between you and me,
Everything is special, day by day,
year by year, life by life.
Just you and me.

You and Me

Don't judge me without knowing me.
Don't criticize my actions.
Don't treat me so harshly.
Don't destroy my soul.
If you do so, you will destroy yourself.
Don't come near me if you don't understand me.
Don't say what you don't mean.
Don't say what you don't feel.
It's better if you don't say a word.
Don't think that I don't know
Everything about you.
We are the reflection without any discussion.
We are twin souls.
You may not agree with me,
But it's true.
Don't hurt my heart because I'm real.
I'm like you; I'm alive, the same as you.
I can feel. And one more thing, please:
Don't pretend that you don't know
How you feel about me.
All I need is to see your eyes, and it's right there.
How you feel, how I feel,
Our love so immense, our love has no end.
Just you and me, just me and you.

Looking for You

Where are you? Where did you go?
I'm looking for you everywhere.
I miss you so much.
If you don't show up,
Slowly, very slowly, I will die
Waiting for you,
Because I still believe in you.
After all, you are not so bad.
I still remember our special day,
The wonderful day when you and me,
With a big smile, made a promise
That you'll never leave and I'll never go.
Please don't break your word—
Or do you want to be free of me?
After all, that is what I see.
You forgot all about me.
Is there any promise
that you can keep with you?
And all you did was lie to me.
How cruel of you, to be like that,
Doing things that killed the love,
Love from me, not from you.
But thank you anyway
For going away.
Because thanks to you, I did learn
How much pain you can receive
From all those that are just like you.
Just like you.

We Believe

If I believe, so can you.
If you can fly, so can I.
If I can trust, why not you?
If I can feel, so can my heart.
If you understand,
Then you know what it means
To love someone.
Someone with an open heart,
Someone who knows how hard it is
To find love, a love who cares.
The love who gives all for you.
The love that is everywhere,
Just for you, when you have needs.
The one who doesn't have any questions
About what you did or what you are.
If you are strong, I'm next to you.
We'll beat the world.
Because we are two in one,
And we will have better thoughts,
And we will see the positive things
In everything that is alive.

All I Say

What can I say?
I have a lot to talk about,
But it's hard to find a way to start.
Do I talk about you,
Or do I talk about me?
It's easy to talk about you,
But it's hard to say something about me.
You are so sweet, so kind, so lovely, so strong,
And so right, and never wrong.
You're perfect in every way.
You are, like I say, the chosen one.
For good or bad, you are the only one.
And me ... it's hard to say, hard to explain.
I don't know what to do; my life sucks.
My body is trash; my heart is wrong.
And all I know is, I could do nothing.
I was not smart; I was not brave.
But thanks to you,
My road changed.
I learned from you, and in the end,
The one who will talk about me
Will be you, not me.
Not me anymore, not me anymore.

A Mistake

If I were you, I wouldn't stay.
If I were you, I would run away.
If I were you, I wouldn't wait.
If I were you, I would say,
"Stop right there."
Stop right there.
You are looking at the wrong place.
You are looking for what I don't have.
I have to go; I have to run.
I can't wait; you must understand.
What's the point?
This is the end between you and me.
As you know, we make it wrong.
You are not for me, and I'm not for you.
I can't give you what you want.
Wrong place for you,
Wrong place for me.

Don't Be Wrong

I'm so sad; I'm so blue.
All I think about is my wish,
Waiting to see if it comes true.
I know it will because I believe.
If you got yours, why not me?
After all, that's all I have,
Nothing else, no more, no less.
All I ask is a small thing—it's no big deal.
Oh magic life, I know you are fair.
I want to wait because I want it so;
That is my only hope.
I know how it looks:
Stupid for you, weird for all.
Oh, blue sky makes me smile.
Between you and me, it won't be like this.
All my life is kind of rare and weird.
Whatever I say sounds crazy, as you know.
Instead of sad, I should be out of my mind,
So it's better to sound crazy than to be sad.
But believe it or not, I'm really sad. I'm feeling blue.
I'm not trying to say it's because of you.

MICHELLE RIVERA (MIKI)

You are not important to me
Because if I think about you,
There is nothing I can feel—it's like you don't exist.
I guess it's just I'm sad. I'm blue.
My heart has love, but not for you.
So don't be wrong. Don't try to be brave,
Because it's not you.
All I know is I'm right here waiting
For something better than you.
I'm so glad it's not you, so glad it's not you.

Can't Forgive You

I can't forget, I can't forgive.
I can't have you, I can't let you go.
I say sorry to you,
But at the same time,
I treat you bad.
Then, I make it up to you,
And after that, I regret it and go back.
When you are so sweet, I'm very upset.
I guess it's not me; it's my other self.
I try to be good, but it's too hard.
I think it is better to understand
That I won't change; I was born that way.
There is nothing to do.
I don't like who I am.
I don't like the way I act.
When you say "I love you," and I say okay.
It may not be right; I see it in your face.
I can see all the love you have for me
I don't deserve.
Maybe no, maybe yes.
But it's so deep, the way I feel.
I keep remembering how often you lied to me
When you became a cheater to me.
And my heart is still bleeding and won't stop
Till I learn how to forgive and how to forget.

My First Love

I'm only sixteen, and you twenty-four.
It's so weird, what I feel;
I don't understand.
Maybe I'm sick, I don't know.
Please, I need help—who can explain?
I don't eat, I can't sleep, I can't think.
All I feel are butterflies inside of me.
Is that good? Is that bad? I want to know.
Sometimes I'm happy; sometimes I'm sad.
I feel my heart beating so fast,
And all I think about is you.
I close my eyes and I see your face.
I see your lips so sweet, so fresh,
And all I want is a warm kiss
And to be hugged tightly,
And a soft, whispering voice
Saying beautiful things in my ears.
But then I open my eyes
And realize it's just a dream.
Because if I'm in love, it's just me, not you.

You might say I'm a little girl
And I don't know the things of love,
But the worst is that you don't know what love is.
And I will never say a word.
For me, you are so far,
Like a star, like a moon, like a sun.
And I'm like a flower,
Like a tree, like a sea, but I'm right here,
Dealing with my heart
And learning about my first illusion,
My first love.

Four Letters

A simple word,
But a beautiful one.
A curious word,
Only four letters.
A unique word,
A soft word.
A magic word,
A priceless word.
An incredible word,
A beautiful word.
A sweet word,
A free word.
An incomparable word,
A word that not everybody knows.
A word that will make you happy.
And the four-letter word is
Love.
Famed word, oh, love.
Love from me.
Love from you.
Love for all.

Dreams

I'm thinking about you
Even when I'm awake.
Is it just a dream?
It must be that.
It's the only way.
I can feel, as if you were next to me;
I can feel your breath on my ear.
Moving my hands,
I feel as if I could touch your warm soul.
When I turn around,
I can smell the scent of your body.
I try to sleep, but I can't
Because I don't know
If I'm asleep or if I'm awake.
And all I know is I am dreaming awake
Until my sweet dreams came true.
I will never stop loving you.

You Are Still Here

Stop—don't say anything.
Let me keep you in my memory.
Day by day, night by night,
I will keep your image in my mind,
So I will feel you next to me all the time
And make me think that you never left.
That is the only way
To make my heart stay alive
And never die.
I know it's not the same.
I know you won't be here.
I know I'll be alone.
But thinking and dreaming of you
Will feel real for me,
Because all that love you gave to me
Will make me feel
You are still here with me.
That's the way I think.
That's the way I feel.

Behind You

What can I do with you?
Love you less? Love you more?
Could I do it?
If I love you less, it'll break my heart.
If I love you more, it'll make me crazy.
I have no choice.
I can't change my love for you.
Maybe I look selfish to you.
It could be that I don't know
How you feel about me.
All I know is I'm here for you,
Now and forever,
Always for you, with an open heart,
For better or worse.
Don't forget, I'm right here in front of you,
Waiting for the day
You turn around and look at me
With all the love that grows in me,
Just for you, just for you.

Thank You

Thanks to you, I'm so brave.
I learned from you how to love.
You showed me the way to forget,
No matter how, no matter who.
You let me be born; you let me grow.
When I almost fell,
You were there for me.
If my road was wrong,
You made it right.
If I got sick, you made me better.
You were always there next to me.
If I got lost, you held out your hand
To help me find the way out.
When I felt weak,
You made me strong.
There is no one like you.
You are all hope; you are all love.
All thanks to you, blessed Lord.
Thanks for all I got from you.
Thank you for a wonderful world.
Thank you, Lord.

Liar

I never thought to cry for you.
I never thought it would hurt so much.
I still remember all your lies,
All the promises you never kept.
How good of an actor you really were.
All those beautiful moments of my life,
All the times that I took care of you.
Now I know I wasted my time just for you.
I treated you like a king, like my king.
I would like to go back
To the day when I found you
And turn around, and stay far,
Far away from you, but it's too late.
My love is bigger than my mind.
Now I just need time, a lot of time,
To take you out, out of my life.

You Will Not Come

It was a cold rainy night.
I was really nervous,
Looking at the clock.
Every time that I heard noise
Coming from outside,
I knew you'd show up anytime.
I thought you forgot what I did.
I thought you didn't remember anymore
The day when I broke your heart.
But you can't just blame it all on me;
Let us be honest and say the truth.
I'm as guilty as you.
The hours are passing really fast.
I guess I'm wrong, and you won't come.
I guess I will say you changed your mind
And decided to forget,
But not to forgive.
I just want you to know
That it is in your hands.
The choice is yours
To come back to me.
And until then,
I will wait right here,
Wasting my life,
Living with hope. As you know,
That is the last one to die.

You Are Not Alone

Don't look for a rich person.
Look for a millionaire,
But a millionaire of love
So you can share it
With the whole world,
With all those who are alone.
Show them the real way.
The real love.
The one we know.
The one they didn't keep.
The one they let go.
The one they don't know anymore.
Show them how to keep
All the love they have in their heart.
They don't know,
So let them know
They are not alone,
And they won't be,
Never more, never more.

You Are the One

When you find the right one,
Don't let it go.
You will know
When you find the one
That's worth keeping,
The one that won't judge
The life that you had before.
Just let your heart pick for you.
Let your heart do the work.
Let your heart do it all.
Remember that in our life,
There is only one chance,
Only one, so don't let it go.
Don't let it go the other way.
It won't come back.
It will never come back.

You Are Nothing to Me

Go away, go away!
I will never miss you anymore,
And my feelings will never
Be thinking about
You breaking my heart.
Like the air I breathe,
You came to me
Silently, without any noise.
In the same way, you came.
In the same way, you ran away.
How many lies will I get from you?
I don't know.
I just know the way you act.
Don't ever think about coming back.
I will never forgive you anymore.
And not only for your attitude;
There are a lot of things.
I will never know how many times
You left me here,
So go away and don't look back.
You are nothing to me,
Nothing anymore
Since the day you went away.
So please don't let me say it twice.
Please, go away, go away.

Your Decision

I'm so proud to be me.
I like the way I am.
I don't regret who I am, or who I was.
I'm not perfect.
I know that, but who could be?
I bet it's not you.
I'm not looking for the perfect one.
I'm just looking for the understanding one.
And I know you are the one,
Or maybe not.
You let me know If I can trust you.
You have the last word.
The answer is yours.
I'll just wait for you.
The question is mine.
What will you say?
Tell me now, yes or no?
Don't take too long
Because I could decide
Not to wait for you anymore.

New Year

I woke up today—
It is a new year—
And I thought to myself,
Thank you, Jesus,
For letting me make it until now
And letting me go for another year.
Especially for letting me know you
Since I was born.
Thank you for living in me
And staying by my side,
And when I need you,
You are right there for me
To hold my hand.
And don't let me fall.

Not Meant to Be

One by one, my tears don't stop.
When you decided to go away,
I never thought that my lonely heart
Would suffer so much.
I knew you would not come back.
I would say it's not our fault;
It was too late when we met.
You belonged to someone else, and so did I.
I know we never meant to hurt our feelings.
The reality is that our love was not meant to be,
And we will continue with our real lives,
You loving me, me loving you.
You with her, me with him, far away,
But having each other in our dreams.
Just you and me.
Just you and me.

Together

We are together on the same road.
Our destinies go the same way.
The world is ours.
We have nothing else to say.
We are close to each other
More and more.
We will be together one day,
Forever and ever.
Our feelings are so strong
That nobody will break it off.
Tomorrow is ours; so is today.
I don't care about the rest of the world.
You are the one who I care about.

I Will Tell You

I want to let you know
All my feelings.
I want to tell you
All my thoughts.
I want you to listen
To my intentions.
Without you, I cannot live.
Without you, I will die.
You meant a lot to me;
That is the truth.
I'm full of love
Just for you.

Same as You

Everybody thinks I'm different,
But I'm not.
I don't care if anyone
Talks about me.
I'm like everybody else.
I am like you, like them.
But I can't change people's minds.
I just know I'm not different.
And I know I have
Two strong hands like you,
A mouth to talk like you,
And the biggest heart
To love anyone.
I may be fat, short, and dark,
Not rich, and possibly not a star,
But I have feelings like you.
Like all those that have a heart and a soul.
Remember, I am not different.
I'm just like any other person.
I am just like you.

Won't Be Afraid

I called you many times today,
But I have no answer.
What is the reason?
You haven't looked for me,
And every time, you avoid me.
Well, let me tell you this:
I won't stop until I find you.
I will never give up.
I love you so much,
And I know you do too.
But you are afraid
To get your heart broken,
Like the last time.
Don't worry.
I'm not like those
Without heart, without a soul.
I am me, the one who is full of love
Just for you.

Go On

Don't look back.
Forget all that you left behind.
Go on, follow your road.
Enjoy what you find.
Don't stop.
You deserve to be happy.
Live the life that you never had.
It is time to fix your heart
And take in all the nice things
That the world offers you.
Go find them and keep them.
Forget the harm
That everybody did to you.
Forgive and forget.
I know this:
You won't regret.

MICHELLE RIVERA (MIKI)

A Real Friend

I will say it is hard and difficult,
And almost impossible.
Who will give you a hand?
The one who keeps your secrets?
The one who is there for you when you need it?
The one who you can trust,
The one who gives you time,
The one who gives up everything for you,
The one who does not judge you
And does not look at your mistakes?
The one who shares your pain
And feels it with you?
The one who never asks
For anything in return
And never pushes you?
The one who sees only your heart?
The one who is there for no reason?
The one who has no name?
The one who is more than family,
More than a brother, sister, father, or mother?
We may call it a friend; the one is hard to find.
The one who gives you respect
And is honest and will give his life
For you anytime, just for you.
The one who is more than a friend,
Hard to find, hard to keep.
Best friend, where are you?
Where are you?
My real friend.

Memories

I always have in my mind
My beautiful childhood.
I remember our poor little house,
But rich in love.
The corner where I was born.
The big hole that was in the wall,
The one that my mother
A window used to call,
Where the sun kept shining through every morning,
Sunshine that always woke me up.
I remember the beautiful paper doll
That my mother gave to me,
And how happy it made me.
And I still feel the pain, and it makes me sad
To remember how the rain came down
When I left it outside one day,
Destroying and taking it away from me.
I remember how much I cried for my doll.
I remember when it was my birthday;
All I had as a gift was my mother's hugs
And a sweet smile that was full of love.
She still is the sweetest mom.
These are memories of my childhood life,
A beautiful, innocent age,
My beautiful memories in time.

Who Are You?

I don't know you. Who are you?
You just appeared in my life
From nowhere one day,
And I don't know what I saw in you.
Could I be wrong?
I don't know you. It has been a long time,
And still I don't know you.
Everything bothers you
In the morning, in the night, at any time.
I don't know you.
I don't have your attention anymore.
I don't remember the last sweet word you said.
I don't know you anymore.
I don't know how to describe you anymore.
I never see you close to me.
Rather than be by my side, you prefer to be away.
I don't know what else to do.
I gave you more than I have,
And you want more than what you deserve.
I don't know you anymore.
It seems like you don't care about me.
You never share a little bit of what you have.

You are so cruel, more and more every day.
I don't know you anymore.
I'm not sure what reason I have
To love you anymore.
I may be out of my mind, or I may be crazy.
I don't know what's wrong with me.
I don't know you; that is all I know.
I don't know you anymore—
Not anymore.

Far Away

You know how much I love you,
But don't think that I
Will be begging for you to return.
I'm not the same anymore.
If you want to leave,
Go ahead. I won't stop you.
But remember, there is nobody like me,
Who loves you like a fool.
And let me tell you,
If you feel something is wrong,
Don't blame others.
Blame yourself.
After all, that was your choice.
If you think that money
Is worth more than love,
Then you don't need me anymore.
Forget about me and be happy.
I wish you the best.
Take my word.
Don't came back
Because I will be on my way
To a place far, far away from you.

Thinking About You

When I think about you,
I start to get nervous.
When I think about you,
I feel you in my heart.
When I think about you,
I know how intense
My love is for you.
When I think about you,
I wish you could be here.
When I think about you,
I have all the memories
In my head.
When I think about you,
I know how special
You are to me.
When I think about you,
My heart beats faster.
When I think about you,
I want to know
More about you.
When I think about you,
My heart suffers for you.
When I think about you,
I don't know what to do
Because I keep thinking
More and more about you.

MICHELLE RIVERA (MIKI)

There Is No Age to Be in Love

I don't care how old you are—
Five years, ten years, or more than me.
Our hearts are old enough to fall in love.
Make your choice; I will make mine.
If we are happy, we can ignore the world.
When others don't understand,
It's better not to explain.
Besides, we don't have to say a word about our lives,
And nobody should care if you love me.
I love you, and that's all we care about.
We will be together to the end,
And with a lot of luck,
The end is very, very far.
So we will have a lot of time to live our love
From our beautiful hearts.
From our beautiful souls.
Our deepest love.

Love

Lord, give me what I'm asking for.
I have yet to find a real love.
Is this a punishment?
Nobody looks at me.
Sometimes it feels like I don't exist.
Lord, take me through the road of love.
This loneliness is killing me,
Day by day.
I can't handle this anymore.
Please, Lord, send someone
To be by my side.
That is all I want.
Let me feel alive.
Let me touch real love.

So Sad

Today I am very sad.
My heart is really upset.
It's not easy to let you go.
I tell my heart to be strong,
But it won't listen to any of my words.
I have to repeat it, a thousand times,
That we must give up
And let you go.
We must understand
What reasons you might have.
But I understand. I'm the same as my heart,
Blind, deaf, and persistent.
But we will work together
And try very hard to forget you,
Or die little by little, day by day,
Sadly trying to understand
Why you decided on this.

I Love You

I love you because you are wonderful.
I love you because you make my days happy.
I love you because you share everything with me.
I love you because you like my opinions.
I love you for all that I get from you.
I love you for you honesty.
I love you because
There is nobody like you anymore.
I love you like nobody else can.
I love you for who you are,
And I love you for what you are.
I love you because it's you whom I love.
I love you with all my soul, with all my soul.

Oh, Mother

Oh, Mother, I can't hold it anymore.
Your absence is so big.
It makes me cry night and day
When I realize that you won't come back.
My heart wants to die.
I need you more than ever in my lonely life.
Oh, Mother, what can I say?
I remember all those beautiful moments
When we talked and laughed without stopping.
Oh, Mother, I'm so sorry I didn't give you enough time.
I wish you would have never gone away.
Now I feel kind of guilty, and I can't forgive myself.
You were part of my life, part of my heart.
Oh, Mother, all I want is to be strong
And keep you forever in my heart.

Shining Star

I can't find a name for you.
It's hard to name someone like you,
But I know you like I know myself.
How to describe you is easy for me.
It's no wonder; you lived nine months inside of me.
I loved you so much ever since I knew you were coming.
It was like reaching a shining star from the sky.
You are my reason to live.
It's you that is keeping me alive.
It's an indescribable love that only a mother can feel.
I still remember when you smiled for the first time,
Your first word, your first tear,
The first time I touched your hand,
Your first kiss that is still on my cheek,
The time of your first step.
All of this I will keep deep in my heart.
You will be the baby of my eyes.
I will love you forever, my sweetheart.
This poem is just for you,
From the deepest part of my heart.

Don't

Don't let me go; don't make me cry,
Don't kill my feelings.
Let me be engaged in your heart.
Let me be the shadow of your life.
Please don't push me away from you.
Ask me to walk next to you.
Let's wake up together every morning.
Let's go and end the day every night.
Let me be the one who occupies your time.
Let me be the only one in your dreams.
Don't let me go, or I will die without you.
Let me spend the rest of my life with you.
Please don't tell me to go.
If I lose you, I won't survive.
Please stay in my life. Be my sun.
Be my moon. Be my star
Because you are all I need.

Sweet Thoughts

My mouth gets so watery
Just by looking at it once.
It makes my head turn around
A thousand times.
My mind goes crazy, more and more.
I can feel its warmth near my nose,
And its sweet taste down my throat.
The smell is strong and sweet.
I think once, I think twice,
And all I know is I can't resist.
Once again, I try to think,
But my addiction is too strong,
And I feel so weak.
My hunger says yes;
My mind says no.
You can see
My sweet thoughts for you,
And believe me, with all my heart,
And with all the sugar in my blood,
I love you as much as I love my warm cookies.
Without my cookies, I will survive,
But without you, I will surely die.

Kisses of Wine

Every hug you give me
Is like being next to the sun.
You are so warm.
Every kiss you give me
Is like a glass of wine;
You make me feel so intoxicated with love.
Every touch I get from you
Warms my body.
Oh my God, I'm on fire.
Every whispered word from you in my ears
Is a love secret.
You make me flush.
Every look from you makes me weak.
Oh God, don't let me fall.
Every time we make love,
You make me tremble.
We are going to have an explosion of love.
Every morning that I wake up by your side,
I say thank you, God.
Thank you, God, for letting me be with you.

Painful Love

You are like a red rose.
You hurt me with only a touch,
But you are beautiful.
So I will be next to you like a tree.
I will be your gardener.
I will be your rain.
I will be your sun that warms you up.
I will be your meal every morning,
The one who feeds you
Whenever you are hungry.
I will be the rain that will kill your thirst.
My fragile flower,
I will keep you alive until I die.
Otherwise, nothing will break us apart.
Both of us know that.
And I don't care if your love is less.
We both know my love for you is enough.

Ghost

Like a ghost,
I walk with you.
Like the wind,
I touch your face.
Like wine,
I kiss your lips.
Like a dog,
I smell your scent.
I know I'm crazy,
But crazy for you,
And I am making poems
Without making any sense
Just thinking about you.

Nice Day

Today is a nice day,
Like some other days,
With the weather hot
And the sun on my side.
Yet I feel so sad
That I want to cry,
And I don't know why.
Life is so short,
And we just don't
Learn how to change
A tear to a smile.
No, I don't deserve this,
But who am I
To fight against you?
I am not wasting my tears
Just for you
If I spend part of my life
Believing in you.

Perfect

Look at those big eyes you have,
Big like your heart,
Big like your feelings.
Looking at you is like finding
The way to heaven
Or like dreaming awake.
How lucky I am.
Could I ask for something more?
Let me keep my eyes closed
And draw your figure in my mind.
That way, all is perfect and right.

What a Day

Oh my, oh my.
What a mysterious day.
I have learned many things.
It's like the first day of my life,
A real, real life.
I learned to see the real color of the sky.
I learned the truth of the stars.
I learned the secret of the sun
And the sadness of the cold,
The freedom of the air
And the beauty of peace
And at the same time
Having you near me.
There is nothing else to ask for,
Because my reality is you,
You, my sweet, true love.
It's just you, just you.

I Am a Song

With my soul destroyed
And my heart enchanted,
My brain tortured
And my memory confused,
I ask myself:
Do I still have a life?
Do I still survive?
How many tears
Do I need to waste?
My eyes complain
Of too much crying.
My hands can't handle it anymore,
So many times trying to pray.
It may not be me;
Maybe I am in the wrong world,
Where nobody helps and nobody cares,
Where their eyes are closed and blind,
Where their hearts are as big as stones.
Or I may go another way;
My life is almost gone
And I don't exist anymore.
If you want to find me,
I am a song, a beautiful and sad song.

No One

Tears are falling from the sky.
The harder the rain is,
The harder the pain is for me.
But as you see,
Every tear of my heart has a price.
How easy it is for you,
Living life lying to the world,
To innocent souls that gave all for you.
I have so much to say about you,
But there is no way
I am going to waste my time.
You hurt me so much.
Enough is enough.
You are not for me.
You are no one.

Christmastime

Now the season has changed;
Before too hot, and now too cold.
And all those windy days and nights will come.
Before they would go to the beach;
Now they go ice skiing.
Soon, Christmastime will be here,
With all your loved ones around,
And all the little ones
Running around,
Getting their favorite sweets
And looking at how beautiful the snow looks
Falling from the sky.
A lot of happy faces
Wait for that special night at midnight,
When the man with white and red
Comes with a long beard
Hanging from his chin,
The one that everybody knows
With different names,
Filling the stockings with gifts
To let us know when Jesus was born.
And the same happiness will come
At the end of every year,
When the old dies and the new are born
And all the world makes a new life.
All we know is the best we can do,
Forgetting and forgiving.
Oh, and don't forget to give me a hug
Is Christmastime.

Be Yourself

Does anybody need words
To express their feelings?
The worst thing is when
Someone doesn't know
How to read the other one.
If you want to know someone's feelings,
Look deeper in the eyes, and you will find them.
If you want to know if someone is honest,
Touch their heart.
If you want to know if someone loves you,
Give them a huge hug and an incredible kiss,
And you will feel it.
If you want that someone to love you,
Be yourself, and don't be
The reflection of anyone else.
Your values are more
When you have a transparent soul.

Sounds of My Heart

Like thunder are the sounds of my heart;
Like a flowing river
My tears are sliding down my cheek.
Like the wind takes the dust everywhere,
Destiny is taking you away.
Like the night, my life is getting dark too.
Like the cloudy day, my hope is disappearing.
Like the freezing weather, my soul will be frozen too,
And there will be no more of me.
And all those beautiful feelings
Become a dream, a sweet dream,
A dream that will heal your pain
And bring you peace.
At least for me,
Love must be without fear.
The abandoned should not be
something to care about.
Like it, say it.

Empty

My body is empty; my mind is open.
My soul is flying; my heart is blocked.
My life is locked, and you don't know
How wonderful it is relaxing.
Try it once, and you will see
The difference when there are
More ways to see the world,
Living inside or out traveling,
Finding out what the difference is.
Seeing places not everybody can go to,
Feeling their presence
Where you and me know
How it feels being free,
Without any consequence.

Real or Not Real?

I can't take one more step.
My hands are tired.
My eyes are hard to open.
My mind is almost gone.
My age is hard to say.
But my heart is still beating
Without understanding.
I am trying to give one more step;
Something tells me
There will be for me an end.
This life did not treat me so well.
Or I may say, this was only a nightmare,
And it's almost time to wake up
And find out what is real,
And what is not.
And if this world is a dream,
And the real one is the other one.

Regrets

How can I forgive you?
After all, you're right.
Nobody cares about me.
I should hate the world
For being treated this way.
But on one thing you are wrong.
I do not give up easy.
My courage is all I need to stand up.
I guess you don't know me very well,
And you will be sorry at the end
For all that you have said.

Payback

Each step of my life
Is a mark that I carry day by day.
Every pain in my heart,
It was not because I wanted it.
Every time that I smiled,
It was real and true.
Every time my eyes would shine,
It was because I knew of happiness.
Every time you lied to me,
You made a hole in my heart,
And I'm not happy with that.
You throw me an arrow
To finish me at once.
Too bad this life is too short
And there is not enough time
For you to pay me back.
Just keep in mind, all that you gave
Comes back, is impossible to escape.
What is for you is for you,
And what is for me is for me.
It is a law of life.

Just Love

When my eyes see you,
My body shakes.
When my hands touch you,
I almost faint.
When my body feels you,
I can't breathe.
When I kiss your lips,
I'm so scared,
Thinking about if this has to end.
I hope none of this disappears
And you and I become
The word of love
And are printed in a card of love
For those who are like us,
Full of love, full of love,
And we all know that real love
Never ends, never ends.

I May Die

I may die tomorrow.
I may die today.
I may die right now.
But for sure what I feel
Will never do.
If I can get a wish,
I'll ask for two:
One to live in you,
And the other to live for you.
But we can't change the rules.
And all we can do is this.
If I die first, my body will leave,
But my heart and soul
Will always be next to you.
For sure, you may not see anything.
But I know you will feel
Something, and that is me,
The one who will always be
In your life, in your dreams.
That is me, just me.

The Avoidable

Lonely is a very sad word,
But we can't avoid it.
Everyone in life has to walk
Under the empty tunnel.
Let's call it that way.
You may say you never did,
But you know the truth.
You may be a princess.
You may be the rich.
You may have everything.
You may be powerful,
And you may not accept this,
But inside you, the loneliness is killing you.
And the same as me,
You would like to be a beautiful bird
And fly and fly all over the world and seas
And not to be alone again.

What I Said

Why should I waste my words
If I have nothing from you?
Why should I spend all my time
When there is nothing
I have received from you?
Why should I throw my life in the air?
But thinking twice, life is short,
And with a lot of pain, I've got to go.
It is so difficult, but we'll survive.
Being close or far is the same.
No matter how I feel, we all know
That this is real.
What I've said is from my heart.

I Can Do It

I can see your soul
By looking into your eyes.
I can sense your feelings
By touching your heart.
I can feel your passion
With only one kiss.
I can reach a star,
If you want me to.
I can bring you the moon
On a dark night, if that is your wish,
Or I can give you a piece of the blue sky.
I can take you through the universe;
You just have to ask.
I can take you to paradise
Anytime you want me to.
I can make a song for you
Describing all of our love.
I can write a book about you,
All by just thinking of you.

Inspired

You are my inspiration.
You are the empty book that I need.
You are the poem of my life;
You make me the best poet.
You are the reflection of love.
You wake up the love in me.
You are my enthusiasm to write.
You are the one who makes me put
Writings from my heart,
All the beautiful words,
In this book of poems.
A book of poems that inspires me in my life:
That is what you are for me.

My Book

Where is my book of poems?
Is it hiding from me?
Does it not want to be seen?
Is it afraid to be read?
Well, hold your worries.
I don't need to read it
Because the poems live in me.
They are my creation;
They are made from my soul,
My heart. They are my feelings,
Made from pieces of my heart
And the rest from my mind.
That is why I don't exist.
I became a book of poems
Without feet, without hands,
But with more feeling than you.
So when you open it,
Treat me with care, with love.

Holding Our Tears

It may be the worst place in your life,
Where you can see compassion, tears, and pain.
Babies, kids, adults, all ages—
Some of them try to hide so much pain,
Showing happiness that is not there.
This is the place where you talk to God,
Where God decides if you have to go
Or if you can stay.
Oh, what a life, hard to understand.
Today we are here, and tomorrow we are gone.
That is God's plan, and before he calls us,
He gives us another chance
To feel compassion at this special place
Called the hospital.
Good or bad, it is our last hope.

Really Hard

It is not until now
That I realized how difficult life is.
A lot to learn, a lot to see,
A lot to hear, a lot to feel,
A lot to do that frustrates us all;
This is the most common way you may feel.
It would be great if we could be born
Understanding life in our heads and in our hearts,
But we don't have that choice at this time,
When we arrive at this big world,
To be less or to be more.
Until we are aware of what is going on,
All we do is work hard to survive
By learning more and more.
But remember we are not the same.
We are all different kind of minds
Contemplating how to deal
With this brain and this heart.

My Close Friend

My close friend is the one who cares for me
And is always there for me.
My close friend is the one who never talks bad about me
And never turns his back on me.
My close friend is the one who gives me a good advice if I am wrong,
And gives a hand if I ever need it.
My close friend is the one who gives me a hug when I cry
And gives up his life just for me.
My close friend is the one who talks to me face-to-face
And listens to me if I need it so.
My close friend is the one who shares in my pain and love,
Whom I trust entirely and who knows if I lie.
My close friend is the one who keeps all my secrets in a special place
And goes with me everywhere.
My close friend is the one I will call my best friend,
And I'm so proud of my best friend.
If you want to know who it is,
It is time to meet my best friend.
Just turn around;
It is me.
I am right here next to you.
I am my close friend and best friend.
You are the only one who can trust in yourself.
Believe me—try it once.

What a Dream

Follow your dreams.
Don't let them go.
Once you have a dream,
Hold it with you.
If your dream is to find a prince,
Don't stop until you find him.
If you trust yourself,
That is enough.
A dream is something
That seems hard to reach.
A dream is like a flying feather
That is hard to catch.
A dream is like kissing someone's lips
Without touching them.
A dream is like hope.
A dream is like being in love with you,
But you don't know.
All dreams are beautiful.
So many never have an end.
That is why I open my heart,
So you will see all my dreams.
And believe it or not,
You are my favorite dream,
And I won't give up, not once.
Not once.

Come On

If I were you, I would not be crying here.
Get up and open your eyes.
The world is with you.
The moon and the sun belong to you.
The music comes out from your heart.
The perfumes of the flowers
Were made for you.
The wind is blowing just for you,
To caress your face.
The stars came out just for you
And put a twinkle in your eyes.
The birds are singing to delight your ears.
This is what you deserve,
Not those who broke your heart,
Who are not worth any of your tears.

The Last Page

Walking, walking, walking.
Don't look back; continue ahead.
It's time to close the last page,
The last page of your history.
Lock the bad memories;
Bury the past.
It is time to start a new book.
Forget about the past.
Believe that you are reborn today,
And choose a better road.
Don't make the same mistake.
Remember, there is only one life,
So why should you waste it like this?
Just kill the past and welcome the future
That comes and matters.

Day by Day

Don't rush; don't run.
Don't just live for tomorrow.
Take your life slowly,
One day at a time.
Enjoy day by day.
Love as much as you can.
Give all the passion you have.
Always be yourself.
Don't act; be real.
Don't break anyone's heart.
Don't count the days;
Wait for it.
And if for some reason
One day you fall,
Don't give up. Stand up,
And you will learn.

Nice Place

The place that I want to live in,
Where my princess grew up,
Where happy birds sing beautiful songs
Every morning until the neighbor wakes up,
This is my Baldwin Park.
It has so many things, some small and some large,
Including people with big hearts.
A scenic view of San Gabriel mountains.
A green park where you can walk and run.
A lovely and peaceful place
With thousands of books to read,
Where we become smarter.
Of course, I am talking about the friendly library.
We have so much to talk about,
But my page is gone and my time is running out.
Just remember, I am talking about
One of the most brilliant places we have,
Kind of small but wonderful.
My beautiful Baldwin Park.

If You Were Me

If you were me, what would you do
With those who kill your feelings?
Would you give them another chance?
Those that break your heart,
Will you forgive them?
Those who took your soul
By slicing your heart,
Those who never doubted cutting you in half
And letting you die slowly and alone,
Those who took away your sleep,
Dying every night and day …
Would you ever give them another chance?
Or do you just forget? What if you forget?
There will be a million changes,
So there is nothing else to say.
For me, there is not a second chance.

You Don't Know Me

You lie to me once, you lie to me twice.
There won't be a third time.
I am not stupid. How could you think I am?
But in case you think that way,
Come and tell me right to my face,
And you will get something from me,
Maybe a word that will get stuck
Like a dagger in your heart.
Or my voice stuck like
An arrow in your head.
So take my advice and leave now.
Be smart, and don't be in my way.
Take somewhere else all your lies,
Your perfect lies.

You are my dreams; you are my peace.
You are my life; you are my sins.
You are my good; you are my bad.
You are my heaven; you are my hell.
You are my smile; you are my tears.
You are my trust and my truth.
You are my toughest; you are my mind.
You are my favorite; you are my only one.
You are my life; you are my death.
You are all I care about,
And because of you, I exist.
You are like me, and I am like you.
We are one.

Think About It

It takes one second to fall in love.
It takes all your life to be unloved.
It takes two seconds to feel the passion.
Within seconds, the passion dies.
It takes no time to forget.
It takes all your life to learn.
It takes only five seconds to make a mistake.
It takes more than a lifetime to regret it
And go back again.
It takes all your life to know your other half,
Or sometimes you never completely do.
It takes nine months to arrive in this world.
It takes no time at all to die.
There are no rules, no time, no age to die.
Once your heart stops, you might not have a chance
To say a word or say goodbye to all,
To you, my lovely one.

Expressing

I don't know why, but I like to write.
I like to write what my mind thinks.
I like to write what my heart feels.
I like to write what others think.
I like to express with words.
I like to describe all the feelings,
Bad, good, I don't know.
For some of you, I'll write a poem,
And for others I'll write a song.
For this and that, I find a way to write something
For living and nonliving things,
For a bird, for a dog, for a butterfly.
To the sea, to the stars, to the sky,
To the sun, to the moon, to the air.
Like a flower, like a tree;
Like a baby or a puppy.
I don't know, but what I do know?
A hundred percent is a book with all the feelings
That you, I, and others have
That I will write about to the end.

Talk About

Please let me talk; don't stop me.
You must know the other me, my dark side.
For the first time, I don't want to hurt someone.
For all I did in my past …
I was a devil with no tail and no horns,
No heart and an empty soul.
I could call myself a black angel
Who turned white, out of nothing.
From nowhere you just appeared,
And you changed my life.
With you, my soul grew.
I found my heart and found my peace.
It is just a story of me—hard to believe—
And what is important is if you believe in me too.

After

After a good day is gone,
A good night arrives.
After the sun runs to hide,
The moon will arise.
After a hard day of work,
I fall in your arms.
During a good night of sleep,
I follow my dreams.
After a peaceful day,
I truly can breathe.
After a beautiful poem,
I can write you a song.
After I tell you a sad history,
Tears fall down your face.
After you came into my life,
I was the luckiest woman in this world.
After I described my feelings to you,
You knew me more than I did.
After I gave you my life,
You gave me more than you had.
After time passes by, we will be two in one.
After our secret is written, spread it to the world
And tell them about our promised secret love.

Sleepless

I close my eyes, but I can't sleep.
I'm still awake,
Maybe because I forgot how to sleep,
Or I am just afraid
That my heart will stop beating.
But what do I do? I need to sleep.
Maybe because I need you next to me,
Or I am not tired enough to rest.
Oh, I want to sleep. How about if I read,
Or take a warm glass of milk?
I am asking myself, why me?
Why did it happen to me?
After all, my mind is clean.
But all I know is
That I can sleep if there is a solution.
I may wait all night to fall asleep.
Please, please, I cannot sleep.
I must go to sleep.

Open Door

Where are you? Are you with me
Or far from here? But why?
You should be here by my side,
Taking care of me. And believe me,
I don't need all your time.
Just some of it. Please stop.
Stop living everywhere,
Here, there, anywhere.
I care so much for you.
Please tell me where you are.
I need to hear from you.
Bring peace to my heart,
And remember always,
My door will be open for you,
Same as my heart.

My Other Half

I want to tell you something,
And I hope you never forget.
You know I am your other half;
I will be loyal as the moon to the sun.
I will never go away from your side.
I am the one who gives more than I have.
If you asked for my life,
Right away I would give it to you.
If you asked me to die for you,
I would do it without thinking.
You are the love of my life.
Never leave me or make me leave.
I am whomever you want me to be.
I am whom you always dreamed of.

Why does love hurt sometimes?
Why does love give you so much pain?
Why is the pain so deep
That it makes you bleed?
And there is no cure
That will help you heal,
And no matter how painful it is,
It is a pain that nobody can see
Because, while you are smiling,
You are feeling a knife stuck in your heart
And you are trying to make it stop.
I believe that sometimes it is hard
To understand what it means.
I know there is nobody in this world
Who has never felt a pain in their heart
Since they fell in love.

Like a Flower

I am like a flower
That will die with no water.
I will surely die without you.
I am like a beautiful rose
That likes to be admired just by you.
Call me crazy—you know I am crazy and it's for you.
As you see, I don't mind to be like you,
Appreciated and lovely for all of you.

Fantasy Life

Our life is a fantasy, an illusion.
We want this world to change,
But we do things with no sense.
We run through life without really thinking.
We make war instead of peace.
Here we are, and we don't know why.
We have lost touch with love and with ourselves.
We have ears, but we don't want to listen.
We should come back to reality
Instead of living a life of fantasy.
We must use our brains
And appreciate what we have.
Two feet, two hands,
Two ears, and two eyes:
That is what we have.
What else do we need
To make our lives more meaningful
And understand why we live this way,
Lost in this life of fantasy?

Mexico's Heart

My lovely Mexico, how far you are.
I know I was so sad when I find out
That I was leaving you behind,
My beautiful country.
How much damage are they doing to you?
Why are they trying to destroy you?
My beautiful Mexico, they want to finish you.
My Mexico, they don't realize how beautiful you are.
You have a lot to give:
Old picturesque cities with big stories.
Hot and delicious foods.
You have such hardworking people and beautiful women.
Many mountains, rivers, and beaches.
Cancun, Acapulco, Cozumel, Tulum.
Oh Mexico, they are so cruel.
Be strong, like you always are.
Remember, Mexico never gives up.
Beautiful Mexico, I carry you inside my heart,
And there is where you always will be.
It is hard to forget about you,
And you are so easy to love.
I never will finish saying what you are,
My beautiful Mexico.

Thinking Like This

When I think about you, I start to smile,
And I feel you in my heart.
When I think about you,
I know how much I am in love with you,
And I wish I could have you next to me.
When I think about you,
My memories come back to me,
And I know how special you are to me.
When I think about you,
My heart beats so hard that
Everybody can hear it.
When I think about you,
I want to know more about you.
When I think about you,
My heart suffers for you,
And I don't know what to do
Because I keep thinking more about you
When the thought of you comes up.

Poison

Don't be mad; don't show your evil side.
If you keep being aggressive,
You are going to be lonely.
I don't like your attitude.
I don't accept how rude you are.
I can't handle it anymore,
So one of these days, those beautiful eyes
Will not see me again.
And the worst punishment you will have
Will simply be loneliness
For rest of your life,
And your killer will be
The strong poison you have.

Like You

I am looking for a love
That can give me his heart,
And without asking questions
Love me with passion.
He doesn't care who I am
Or where I'm coming from.
He doesn't criticize me
And doesn't count my mistakes.
He never asks where I've gone or done.
He doesn't ask for too much.
Someone who I can trust,
Someone to hold my hand
As we walk in the park
And treat me as if we are still dating,
Who writes a poem for a romantic song.
A love I can see a scary movie with
And hugs me until the movie ends.
Someone who wakes me up every morning
And gives me flowers on my birthday
And makes love to me, day and night.
Someone who, every day,
Loves me the same way I do:
A love like you.

I Don't Know

I don't know what I am looking for.
I don't know what I want.
I don't know what I have.
If I look for it, I can't find it.
If I want it, I can't have it.
It's like being in love
Without having you,
Or having you without loving you,
Making peace with your heart
So it's much better having you.
Loving you and keeping you
Without hurting you.

Wherever You Are

Rocks or mountain, it is the same.
This, that, or the other one, I don't care.
Fakes and liars are all you learn.
Bridges, hills, or rivers
Are all the same for me.
Slow or fast, I don't know.
Same or different, positive or negative.
I can't handle it anymore.
If you come to me on time,
I know you will find me.
If you take too long, I won't be here.
That is how I feel.

Hard to Avoid

You are cold like the snow,
Hard like a rock.
You are impossible to avoid.
You are my wrong way.
You are like dirty water
That nobody wants to touch.
You are like a poisonous plant,
And I want you far from me.
You are the worst enemy;
That is why nobody wants you close.
Sorry to say this,
But that is my way to explain it.
It must be hard to understand
You are all that and more,
But I better stop this now
Or we will start a war.

The Way

You looked at me.
You talked to me.
You were hot like fire,
And I was quieter than silence.
I was free like the wind,
Strong like a storm.
I was with an unforgettable smile.
I was hiding the blushing
Of my face inside my soul.
No matter the reason for our union,
Our love was enough.
That was the way,
We promised each other.

Is It Magic?

Magic, bad luck, or witchcraft? Who knows?
In this world, there will always be
Some things you can't avoid,
Like being in love for the first time.
Love is like magic; it is like an addiction.
Without it, life is meaningless.
It becomes part of you
Like the blood in your heart,
Forever, until you are gone.

 Crazy

I love you like I am crazy.
I adore you like an idiot.
I can't use my brain.
It doesn't let me think.
I want to write a poem, but I can't.
I try to write a song,
And it only gets worse.
Thanks to you, I lost my poetry.
But I want to ask you something.
Will you stay with this idiot?
You will never find another crazy woman
That loves you like I do.
Or right now, you are gone?

Letting You Go

Give me back my heart.
You treat it without compassion.
Give me back my kisses.
They don't belong to you any longer.
I want my poems back.
They are not about you anymore.
I want my pictures back; you no longer care.
Give me back all my belongings.
Don't miss a single thing.
I don't want to see you, hear about you,
Or be with you anymore.
And if you don't believe me, well, I don't care.
All of this hurts my feelings,
and you know it's not my fault.
I'm letting you go; now you can be free.
I really feel sorry for you,
But there is nothing I can do.

You Are My Reason

You are the reason for my life.
You are my motive to live.
You are what I need to exist.
You are the air that I need to breathe.
You are in my heart,
And it's hard to take you out of it.
You are the water that I need to survive.
You are the blood in my veins.
You are my war and peace; you are my soul.
You are the sound of the wind; you are all I feel.
You are the inspiration for my poems.
You are my own body; you live in it.
You are food that fuels my body.
Like vitamins, you give me strength.
I am so grateful for life.
You are the owner of my thoughts and much more.
I love you so much.

Happy for You

If you are happy, I am happy too.
If you cry, I will have tears too.
If you suffer, I will have pain too.
If you are sick, I will do all I can to comfort you.
If you die, I will die with you.
If you are reborn, I will come back with you.
If you take me back, I will be there with you.
If you are happy, I will be happy for you too.
If you change your mind,
I will accept it, and I will walk away from you.
If that is your decision, I will do it for you.

Today

Today is the day.
Today I'll get up with the right foot.
Today is my day.
I will let you get inside my soul.
Today I want to share with all of you
All that is close to my heart.
Today, I want to let you know something
That you may or may not know.
Today, I feel the calm, and I feel free like the wind.
I feel the clouds and the warmth of the sun,
And your advice I am going to follow.
I don't care if you are wrong; I won't say a thing.
Today, I will make all your wishes come true.
I will be an open-minded person.
Today, I don't care who talks about me.
Today is one of those days
When I want to run away,
And I just let my thoughts fly.
Today is not like any other day;
There is nothing that bothers me today.
Today is an unforgettable day.
I feel stronger today from right to left.
Today is today, and today
Is a new day to live, love, and laugh.

My Little Crystal Doll

Where are you? Where are you?
I am looking everywhere for you,
And I can't find you.
Where are you?
Why aren't you here with me?
I am so worried about you.
How fragile you are.
Where are you, my sweetheart?
My crystal doll, my only one,
My sweet love, I will find you.
Whatever it takes, it just takes time.
I don't know, but sooner or later,
You will be here with me.
I know you will. I know you will.

Come to Me

I feel you are my destiny.
I want you; come to me.
I want to be with you
And slowly feel your lips close to mine.
I want to taste you.
I want to make you happy.
I want you to make me happy.
Take me to heaven.
Hold me in your hands,
Tight to the end.
Kill me with your passion.
I want to see your smile.
I want you to come to me,
And let's walk down the same road.
I want you to burn me with your passion.

Three Wishes

If I could have three wishes,
I would ask the sky for you to appear in my life.
To the sea, I would ask for a pearl.
To the wind, I would ask to take it to you.
And to the garden,
I would ask
For an abundance of flowers
To make a crown
Just for you.

Slave

Every love has a history,
And it makes you feel the glory.
Every kiss is a verse;
It always takes you across the universe.
Every night is a poem,
Like the love you feel for me.
Every word from you
Is a kiss for my ears.
When you say you love me,
It is a song for my soul,
And each poem you invent
Makes my heart cry.
But every night, you are in my mind,
And I'm not able to sleep.
My feelings for you are really strong.
I am happy to be
Your love slave.

Terrible Night

It is a long night.
I should think twice.
It is a nightmare.
I want to sleep.
This is too much for me;
My body needs a bed.
What is going on?
I had no idea
It was going to be like this.
This liquid makes me so sick.
I know it's for my own good.
Well, we will find out tomorrow
When the sun comes out,
And you will be here caring for me.

Love for Money

You told me you loved me.
You told me I was the only one,
And I believed you.
Now the time has passed,
And you forgot about it.
There are no more promises.
Now you care for somebody else.
I guess you exchanged love
For a fancy life.
But don't worry about me.
You hurt me so much,
But I'll never hurt you.
Let's see if money makes you happy
And gives you love,
Or if your life becomes
A big lie.

Show Me the Way

Show me the way to love.
Take me step by step,
Holding my hand.
I am so desperate;
I feel lost.
But if you walk with me,
I will feel protected.
You make me feel strong,
But don't take me wrong.
I just want the both of us
To meet love at the same time
And have an unforgettable experience
In our lives.

Stupid Heart

At night I think about you,
And I can't sleep.
During the day I cry for you,
And I can't smile.
The time passes—hours,
Days, months—
And I'm still without sleep.
After the years,
I keep crying for you.
Summer comes
And summer goes,
And I am here, crazy,
Thinking about you.
I know it's hard to believe,
But the only way
To take out my feelings
Is by taking out
My stupid heart,
Which never listens to me,
And becoming the blind
Of this world.

I Am Nervous

You have beautiful eyes and lovely lips.
You make me nervous
When you look at me.
I go crazy at every kiss
I get from you.
When you stand in front of me,
I feel my heart beating fast,
And I want to give you a warm hug,
Like those that you never forget.
You are lovely, my sweetheart.

Same

If I could sleep with the same amount
Of love that I have for you,
Then I would sleep for an eternity.
If I ate the same way I love you,
Instead of walking,
I would roll like a ball.
If I took showers
With the same amount
Of the love I have for you,
I would shine like a beautiful star.
Oh my God, oh my God,
That is what we are.

The Past

All of us have a past,
Some good and some bad.
And I don't understand why
We always remember the bad.
We are so hard-headed
That we don't learn
And will suffer again and again.
Sometimes, when we are on the ground
And we want to give up,
We still manage to get up
And start living the present
Or the past will never end.

After All

After all the love I gave you,
You are gone again.
You forgot about me.
After all I shared with you,
You left me alone.
After all that I lost for you,
You pay me like this.
After you made me think
That you were all mine,
You're finished with me.
After I swore my love for you,
You hurt me like this.
After I looked out after you,
You take away my happiness.
After I sacrificed everything for you,
You push me away without care.
After I showed you all my feelings,
I will never beg you again.

Where Are You

It is impossible to find you.
I looked everywhere I know.
I will find you one day.
I look for you in the seas,
But I can't find you,
And I start to cry.
I call you from the mountains,
And I don't hear an answer.
I look for you
Throughout the city,
And you are not there.
Where are you hiding?
I am knocking door to door,
And you are not there.
Oh, my—finally I realize
I will never find you,
No matter how long
I keep looking for you.

Don't Trust

Like a good friend,
I am going to tell you:
Be careful with those
Who say they are your friends,
Because sometimes
They put stones in your road
And make you fall.
They want to get what you have.
They don't show you their real faces.
They give you a smile
Before putting a knife in your back.
Remember, not everybody
Is to trust.

Believe It

Shoot me; finish with me.
Take out my heart.
Take out my soul.
Destroy my life.
Cut me in half.
Don't have mercy.
Treat me like a slave.
Let me feel a lot of pain.
I accept all of this,
But don't take away
Your love from me
Because without you
I'll have no life.

You Are

You are invisible, like the wind.
You remind me of what I feel.
You are transparent, like water.
That is why I can see
The feelings in your heart.
You are a morning star
That shines at my window
To brighten my days.
You are like a full moon
That makes you feel inspired and at peace.
You are what you are.

Unwanted

I don't know why I'm here.
I don't know why I was born,
Or if nobody was waiting for me.
I was an unexpected baby,
And for the things of destiny
I was abandoned.
Could that be the reason
That I was born?
I don't understand.
Not expected, unwanted,
And abandoned,
I am so grateful for life.
I have the sky as a roof,
And my house is the universe.
And as a gift, I write books
With feelings of love, but the best of this is
I have a God as a friend.

It Hurts

It is so painful; it hurts so much
That I can't help you.
I can't do anything for you.
It hurts a lot just looking at you.
I feel sorry seeing your eyes full of tears,
So destroyed, full of sadness,
Not showing your smile.
Seeing how beautiful you are,
There is nothing to say.
Let me wipe your tears
To make you feel better.
That is all I can do for you.
Here is my shoulder.
I am your support
And always will be.

Without Precaution

I gave you my heart;
You know I am right.
Your soul I got from you,
The one I keep with devotion.
You did not take care of my heart
The right way.
You dropped it, breaking it
Into a million pieces.
Now my heart is everywhere.
Each piece has been stepped on over and over.
I wish I knew magic,
To be able to fix my heart without a scar.
Piece by piece, someone will bring
My heart back, and I will exchange it
For a new love that will be treated with devotion.

Poet of Love

When I write a poem,
It is because of what I have seen.
When I write a story,
It is because of what I have lived.
When I write the truth,
It is because I am honest.
When I write a song,
It is because it comes
From my heart.
When I write a poem,
It is because it comes
From my soul.
When I say I love you,
It is because I really mean it.
When you see me crying,
It is because I need to be hugged.
If sometimes I am sad,
Please make me forget it.
Thanks to the feelings
I have for you,
I have become a poet of love.

Rain or Tears

Rain or tears, you will never know.
Peace or war, you will let me know.
My heart is soft; my soul is strong.
Do you understand what I mean?
I am not the cause of your mistakes.
To accept our errors takes time.
Because of you, my tears are more abundant.
Whatever you do, you blame it on me.
Good or bad, it is always my fault,
And I don't know what to do.
I hear my heart that says to stay.
And my mind says to go
Far, far away from you.

Human Dog

Who is the one who loves me so?
Who waits for me and smiles to me?
You are the only one.
Who cares for me and listens when I speak?
Who worries for me if I get sick,
And who sees my tears if I cry?
You are the only one.
Who will never protest what I say,
And still receive me with a happy tail
And has the time to stay next to me?
You are the number one.
My biggest friend, my loyal, friendly dog.
My human dog, my little thing—
That is what you have been called.
My little thing.

Looking for You

It was early in the morning.
Still, it was a little dark when I found out
That you did not come to sleep.
I got so worried that I decided to go out
And look for you.
I was so nervous that I forgot my shoes,
Walking with my bare feet all over the cold, wet grass
With my body shaking and my hands freezing,
Trying to walk faster and going out of my mind.
And all of this is because of you.
I know if I don't make it back,
It will be on your conscience
Because I did it all for you.

All I Am

They call me crazy
Because I love you.
They call me stupid
Because I can't live without you.
They call me an idiot
Because I talk about you day and night.
They call me dumb
Because I keep thinking about you.
They call me an imbecile
Because sometimes I cry for you.
There is nothing I can be called
To make my mind change;
Accept me being in love.
You are mine, and I am yours.

For the Rest of Your Life

I am your princess; I am your queen.
I am your slave; I am your wife.
I am whatever you want me to be.
I will be your friend,
Your girl, to the end.
Maybe I am your shadow
For the rest of your life.
I hope it doesn't bother you,
Because I am planning
To be with you forever.
I am going to be the dream of your life,
The one who always
Occupies your heart, your mind.

Am I Dreaming?

Today I woke up
Thinking of my dream.
What is happening?
Why are you in my dreams?
Word is that I am falling in love.
Oh, no—what am I saying?
What am I talking about?
How do I dare?
Am I really in love?
For the rest of my life,
Should I hide my feelings in front of you?
Would I be strong enough?
Could I survive without you?
Would you feel the same as me?
My heart is suffering, slowly dying.
We both know we don't belong together.
But anyway, this is just a dream,
An impossible dream.

You and Me

You and me together,
We find the love.
We are our destiny.
We don't need to say anything.
We don't need to talk.
In silence, we read each other's minds.
We know the world is ours.
There is nobody else around;
Only our love is what counts.
Nobody hears when our hearts talk.
Nobody sees what our minds are doing.
We don't have a past;
We might not have a future.
We have today,
And we don't care.
There might be a reason
Why we are here.

Bad Taste

You left a bad taste in my mouth
When you yelled at me
And told me to go away.
I never thought
That I was going to say this:
You are doing me a favor.
Why are you still here?
What are you waiting for?
I want you to go.
I want to be in peace.
I can't stand your presence anymore.
Go on and do your life
Anywhere but here. I don't care.
I never want to see your face again.
Thank you.

Who?

Who am I? I hope you know.
Am I good or bad?
Am I short or tall?
Am I fat or thin?
Who am I? Can you tell?
Am I intelligent or dumb?
Am I brave or a coward?
Am I beautiful or ugly?
Am I worse or better?
Am I nice or terrible?
Who am I?
Am I a ghost or just a soul?
Am I a pencil or a book?
If this is right,
What are you waiting for?
Go on—make a verse, a poem,
A sad history, a novel.
Make your life
Part of the story.

Margarita

Far you can be; many years can pass.
Unmerciful is the distance for separating us.
Though we can't control the distance,
You always are in my mind.
I hope someday to visit you,
And for hours just talk
Of all the things we missed
And need to catch up.
I love you, sister.
This poem is dedicated to you.
No matter how far you are,
You are always close to my heart.

www.ingramcontent.com/pod-product-compliance
Lightning Source LLC
Chambersburg PA
CBHW052023070526
44584CB00016B/1881